Robert James Davies has been writing poetry since the age of fifteen. He has grown with his writing and has been sharpening his craft ever since. He aspires to touch others with his words. *Ana's Hymns* is his first published book.

To Ana, my muse, my life. If it wasn't for you, this poetry book would not have been written.

Robert James Davies

ANA'S HYMNS

AUSTIN MACAULEY PUBLISHERS™

LONDON • CAMBRIDGE • NEW YORK • SHARJAH

Ordering Information
Quantity sales: Special discounts are available on quantity purchases by corporations, associations, and others. For details, contact the publisher at the address below.

Publisher's Cataloging-in-Publication data
Davies, Robert James
Ana's Hymns

ISBN 9781647500320 (Paperback)
ISBN 9781647500313 (Hardback)
ISBN 9781647500337 (ePub e-book)

Library of Congress Catalog Number: 2020925354

www.austinmacauley.com/us

First Published 2022
Austin Macauley Publishers LLC
40 Wall Street, 33rd Floor, Suite 3302
New York, NY 10005
USA

mail-usa@austinmacauley.com
+1 (646) 5125767

Sacred

Once upon in my life,
I was alone then fortune came to be.
You came into my life in a mere interlude.
Smiled,
Gave me your blessing beauty
that gave me
challenges, infinity awake, love awake
So that I may once again be astounded
Give praise to this God's dream,
that love I am living always
I am yours, this I know.
I am immortal, this will never change.
My love will never die
Forever
We are like what we speak to one another and feel
That's what gives wonder, birth to change,
Enrich our lives
Come in a mere second
An emotion is born so we are upon this earth
We have found our place, we are sacred to God.

The Hour of Men

The hour of love is in men's heart,
It still lives, the day is at hand.
We can believe in the dream that we thought was dead.
The powerful gift that we can be one
The hour of peace
when the shadow that was cast in men's hearts,
We have been delivered to God, to America.
The day is here and now
when no more blood shall be spilled for lust of power
or hatred
the beast has been tamed by the symbol
that we always keep sacred, dear to our hearts
the hour of the poets is kept
finally the words are understood
cherished by all.

Rain Man

I am a mirror to the world, with no reflection.
A lie to man, a man that casts no shadow in
the generosity of humanity,
The rain man hanging on to what he has left of hope
walking hand in hand with his disappointment to himself.
He covers in his disguise
to find some sort of integrity to call his own.
Rain man can't find his way to that place of
someone loving him,
always casting out his demons.
Rain man looking inside of himself to finally touch
And understand what he is feeling clouded in mystery
he can't die to release his pain.
He has many times died because it is so hard to find beauty
when the world is so ugly to the rain man.

To My Worship

To my worship,
this I give all my comforts to you.
I renounce all, for you are my pleasures.
You give me creation as my life
for my worship, enticing fragrance of love.
I ask the Lord to grant me no happiness
or the gift to have life for you my worship
you are to my worship
I only know you have been given to me from above.
We are a pair to nature.
To my worship, whisper to make me alive.
Ever after
To all my senses shall you be in the most
vital, beautiful love of my days.

Ego of Men

A man is only a man
but is he equal to God?
Lives are ever-changing
Such are people,
our destinies ever woven
in our belief that we can love one another.
That we can be without sin, without the lust to be superior.
Can man lie within himself
to seek out what is truly called humane?
The foulest murder is that we kill off our unity,
because fear has taken mankind.
We now lose the gift within ourselves.
We forget why we are here.
One voice is heard until another,
another is recognized.
Then we are equal to one another, to God.

Righteous Love

Exist in the name of love I do.
Call me, I will come feel me in your heart.
I will live sickness, in doubt, in yourself
I will give you piece of mind, sadness, fear;
I will give you comfort for we walk as one.
My true love, side by side forever,
through the sun and the rain.
We exist, one soul, it shall be this.
Where ever I shall be,
you shall be my purpose;
why I laugh, cry.
You shall be there,
for I am righteous only because of you.

In This Life

I love you;
if I can't love you in this life,
then it will be in heaven.
I want to believe that
I am yours, that my world is alive.
Because you touched me.
I can be anything without question in this life,
I don't have to suffer, cry;
only you have the power to stop the earth and time
from exciting
I shall go on loving you as long as I show affection
the gift of feeling as God allows me to love you.

Honestly

Honestly, I shall never stop dreaming of you as
long as I live.
Honestly, I will keep you,
build my world around you
spirit, you always move me high into our days.
Honestly, what am I without you:
a lie to the earth, to my truth,
always I will ever be.
Honestly, your kiss is my breath
to go in my life,
to shine within my hopes and dreams.

Today

Today, my eyes opened to realize that I'm not the only one
that matters.
Today, I cried and felt for another person.
I stood alone from myself.
Today, I looked up and understood the beauty in the world.
I have been walking around in a daze, my mind set on me.
I have lost all the important qualities.
I have come to my senses.
Today, I stood in a crowd, sang for Jesus.
Today, I held an infant and was moved within myself.
Today, I spoke to God, understood the meaning.
I am loved.
Today, I sat with a poor man.
I gave from myself to touch a life,
to become important, acknowledged, that all people matter.
We all should have ourselves to heal,
change the world for the better.

You Are Important

You are important to me as prayers to God.
Respect to you as in the glory to the earth.
Every feeling that changes me to touch your life.
You are important to me;
you are my existence,
and you are love.
Love that I know is a gift,
a way of keeping our lives immortal.
You are important to me as laughter is to healing;
music to comfort the pain.
You are the seasons, all the fragile secrets of a woman.
You are important to me as wonder is to women.
I am timeless when I am with you.
Heaven opens up, once again I praise you
For giving me
your love.
You are important to me as my feelings are to you.
I am important to your life,
we are important to the world.

To My Life

This is for you, my life,
that I am speaking to this day.
I give you my heart and everything
that I shall call true, meaningful, while I am with you.
This life, we don't know what the days will bring
but this we know: we shall be together
no matter what we shall experience,
my life, you're my celebration of life.
To be with you, I awake to all we know we know we have
that is sacred.
Our memories, the births of our children.
The tears we shall shed for our losses,
the tender moments that shall comfort us, rebuild us,
make us strong to persevere all the hardships.
This I speak to you gentle.
My only love that shall always be the only thing,
that I shall know as my home.
Even if the world turns away from me.
I shall always have you to come to.
My ambient love.

Call Me by Name

Call me by name,
I am the world that has come from ruins.
Your name is messiah of my life,
that is refuge from pain.
We are called prayers,
that consoles, inspires us.
Call me salvation from darkness
that I take turn to your hope.
Call me eternal
I shall know that you are precious to me.
Call us life, let us know we are important for all time.
I call you love, my blessing.
Call me soul as I call your name, gift from God.
Call me into your dreams,
my enchantment of my heart.
I call you master, my beginning to a whole new life.

Tommy

I am a man who is of words
but I could never put in words
Love you, Tommy, I carry on your name,
I seem to drift apart from what you taught to me.
How much we meant to each other.
I can't go on blaming heaven,
then your memory is dishonored.
Tommy, as I live on in every season,
anybody I love, there is a piece of you.
The memories shall never fall to pieces,
lose the meaning of how important your love was to me.
Tommy, I know I will never find anybody
that will touch my life like you have, Tommy.

Children

Children in this I envy,
I adore them, the builders that come after us,
the new generation that changes the world.
There it is, the magic of youth, untainted innocence;
so we all are, it's where we all start,
before we know how or where our lives will change,
but we always deal with pain
that our tears are comforted by our parents.
The new door is opened, reality sets in,
we fall in love, build a lifestyle we come to know.
We all revert back to that time,
when we are alone in doubt of ourselves about the future.
Be as it my only
in our minds we are children,
that bridge burns very quickly
like a warm memory
so are our lives
such is youth.

I Know You

I know your face
for I walked with you many times in a dream.
I know of hell
to live with no chance of truly being loved.
I know your name
For it is you I only bow to
you are all that I shall perish to,
my cup is full of days that I now can shine through.
You are the one who shall save me
in all the ways a person can be saved.
You favor me in laughter, carry me in your tears.
Women, for you are God's gift of enlightenment,
I can never repay.
Beautiful in many ways
an enchantment that not even God can make more perfect.
If this be a dream,
never shall I awake,
never shall I be more in God's smile.

Find in You

I have been given life when there was no life.
I bear my cross that is heavy.
I was made to believe I was unfit to live.
I felt all emotion go out of me,
I was not a man or a child but a ghost on the horizon.
I never knew of beauty, how to cherish it,
at a standstill in my life
then there was you
who took notice to my tears
did not laugh or mock them.
Gave hope when no hope lived in me.
You mended me when I was broken
gave wealth to my barren world.
Listen to me, my companion,
who has given tenderness to the unloved,
a choice to be your life.
True always is my home that I find in you.

Partner in Love

She is love in the simplest form.
All the elements that surround me.
Breathe, mother of creation, lay with me
my partner in love, that oversees my dreams
makes my wishes come true.
There is no life without you, companion from the heavens.
At night when the world sleeps,
I embrace you, child of my heart.
There is nothing more evident of beauty than you.
On these words I stand true to you.
I shall never leave you, emotion of love.
My foundation of faith. it is you,
you are my breath that makes my life profound
with all your beauty, charms of a woman.

Celestial Love

Only in your heart shall I dwell forever,
it's God himself I pray to keep you in my life.
Only in your heart
there is no question of morality or sacrifice.
My celestial love, it's I alone that I shall beg,
surrender to you.
I shall die in your arms
to prove you're everything I choose to be.
Celestial love, you're the way to paradise,
you're my being,
the fire that burns deep in our infinite love.

For Love

It's for love that I wish for
change in mankind,
I walked with the people of the slums.
Living in doorways of their lost dreams.
It's for love that men build
from the devastations of war.
The cries of the hungry shall be comforted.
The blood-stained slate shall be cleaned by
the revelation of peace.
Love men who walk in the shadows,
the light of enlightenment shall find them
and the world will rejoice for love.
I can walk with no shame
I can trust look into the eyes of men
who I can admire,
call my heroes,
my leaders.

The Question

What is love? Is it God?
If so, can I touch God?
Talk to the father,
see the answer to the infinite question?
Who are my brothers?
Are all men my brothers?
If this is so, why have I not found them yet?
Who am I, I ask the question?
What is life, the profound,
I search, look into the unseen world for the answer?
Can I make a difference, can I touch a life?
What is beauty,
is it something that lives inside of us
but we choose to create it or destroy it?
Can there be peace in the hearts of the children of God?
This I ask, it's for men to answer.

Adrienne

Put love into a name,
or a face to God,
it would be Adrienne.
Try to hold on or catch a rainbow,
it's impossible.
But when she loves you,
never ever will you find such a feeling of
home in your heart.
For she is the one, a woman favored by angels.
Adrienne, come to be my dream come true.
Never leave me, I will always be yours.
I call you my life, the reason I was put into this world.
Fragile, your delicate beauty.
Walk with me, I walk with you, with God.
I love you, my light.
Our names for all time, the world shall know,
Adrienne.

Beyond Eternity

From within we live.
We are meaning the beginning.
Love the quiet I whisper into your mind.
I know then what it is to be born into your life.
How full my heart can be.
Take me now my breath
I shall show you what our lives shall be
love me beyond eternity
love me.

Love's Eyes

Speak, I am poor, starving in myself.
What is love, am I worthy of it?
The only feeling I ever knew was shame,
because I could not be a man that could be loved
or have the gift to be befriended.
You took me into your heart,
gave me understanding to my pain
generosity to care for me.
You slept with, me drove away my curse that haunted me.
You are what I call my life,
my room isolated, barren from my joy,
the curtain has come down.
Love's eyes cover me
light of my hope streams in my soul.
In you, I matter,
you are rest that I have long been denied.
You are my seasons that I can be touched, embraced.
Love's eyes,
I was dead but now I live within you.
Home, I have come home from being lost to all.
Understand me my virtue.
Look at me, you call me your own, with no doubt.
We live together, that is our truth.

I shall never leave your side, nor you, me.
Love's eyes, all that was not,
now I am in love's eyes.

Your Hope

When I can no longer be gentle to you,
we walk separate paths,
that is when it's over.
When I lose my reason to hold you
until all has fallen away
that is when it's over.
When I can no longer hunger for your touch
that is when I know I turned my back on heaven,
I don't have no more feeling or right to love you.
When I can no longer come close to resemble a man
that is when it's over.
I would be a fool to squander my gift to tempt faith.
Only in fairy tales I believed
love reigned supreme,
but I fell into the favor of your heart.
You are my light,
guiding me through the tunnel to your hope.

Passages of Time

Passages of time,
I have come through so much
it's so hard to fathom or live with it anymore.
At times I dreamt
that I was a person who had a richness for life.
I have eaten from the street,
I was alone in the cold bitterness
that became what I lived, stood for, it was my life.
The world will go on regardless of my existence.
Passages of time,
I have worn out my clothes, sores that engulf me.
The loneliness, my only companion that I carry around
in my pocket of old sympathetic memories.
Passages of time,
I reach out to my specters of my past,
the only friends to me beside the darkness,
as I am bound on my journey
down this road that has no end.
My stone inside of me, is heavy.
I live out of matchboxes that I know only as my survival.
I wonder about Jesus, did he die for me?
If nobody loves me, or calls me friend,

he is my friend.
I see myself, the image that I have of me.
A king in a poor man's disguise,
even though the sun does not give me warmth.
The stars that I speak my wishes to,
have fallen from the sky.
I have still my gifts that ease my load.
The gift of laughter,
the gift of mercy that gives life of my prayers,
and my love to all that is my best friend,
my savior as well.

If I Matter

If I matter, will someone comfort and understand me?
Can I be loved by God?
In his image we are all made.
If I matter, will there be a day
when I don't cry my life away, because I am judged?
If I matter, can I be important in somebody's life?
It would be so fine to eat of the finer things in life.
If I matter, could I dream I am important,
as love is to humanity?
If I matter, could I share,
make a difference to express emotions
that maybe could save or create in someone's life?
If I matter, would I be remembered in words or in tears?
If I matter. could I make my pain cease?
I can live my life to know joy
or cry not for sorrow but in happiness.
I have many celebrations inside of me.
If I matter, all I can ask is for someone to give,
to know me as part of humanity.

Love of My Life

It's now, love of my life,
that I'm once again making love to you.
Love of my life,
can you hear our hearts speaking?
It's like heaven once again blessing our lives.
Love of my life,
we are unity recognized by God's love
I see into your soul
I feel you once again
touch me once again
I am here with you
I love you so
love of my life, my unfounded immortality.
Love of my life,
stay inside of me
it has come to pass our love we live
our happiness shall be a flower that shall never wither
or lose its fragrance
love of my life, my eternal love.

For Myself

All my life I have been chasing a shadow
something I saw myself to be
maybe a beautiful rainbow
or something so simple as a star in the sky.
I was always looking for feeling in people.
The river that flows within me
I am waiting for it to reach the sea
to be happy – something in me.
I can be a symbol or sorrow
dark reaching into people's minds
just to be able to feel or really be loved.
I've looked into many streams
I have grown in my years
saw beauty, devastation, heard the cries of the wind.
I looked into many faces
I saw myself
I saw the birth the world that I live in.

Greatest Happiness

The greatest happiness is you, angel of my lifetime.
Before my eyes close, I shall love you.
I will stand in God's presence, tell him of my life,
and the greatest happiness I have found with you.
I still have your tears, warm, soft,
in quiet memories of my mind.
Even when you are away from me,
a ghost locked away in my soul.
You live in your sweetness,
always there is a part of you,
not even death has power over it.
All the secrets of your love are sealed within my lips.
Without you there is no understanding or any feeling
of happiness.
The symphony of the angels rings out in the wind,
to remind me that you are my essence of love,
my greatest happiness.

The Salt of Men

Men, grains of salt that are the earth.
Love me for I am a child of God.
Fingers on the pulse of a generation,
inherit the kingdoms that we shall leave for our children.
We are not forever, like the earth or the sky.
Men are the wind, ever changing in course.
We are important to each other,
like the seeds in the hands of God.
Our devotion, many rays of sunlight.
We grow new nations, flourish by love.
Each life, countless drops in the complex ocean
that makes us humane to one another.

Cease

When we part of for the end of the day
to be renewed in your wake,
I cease to live.
All has halted until you console my life.
I drown in the brown pools of your eyes.
At a stand-still, I am lost in a passage
of a memory that I must indulge on.
An unforgotten truth that has loved me
my spring everlasting
you shame the lips of the angels that control the seasons of
heaven
for you console me a sweet temptation that leads me to
surrender to your comfort.
We chase the breeze far into eternity
that everlasting taste that time has no bearing on.
Cease no more
the passion that is my well
that shall never run dry
my youth shall always be sustained for your body
your truth makes it so
the dreams of my poetry shall never cease to find rhyme

I shall never cease to love you
then I would truly be dead.

Love Evermore

For you,
I promise hope,
I promise life.
For you, my friend,
I promise to be with you forever.
I can't hide my feelings that you give flight to.
I can only cherish you, worship you,
you are as vital to me as God is to heaven.
Everything that has meaning in the universe you are
responsible for.
Alone, sometimes we are,
then we awake, so be it,
you are there again
it begins my life.

Teresa

A comfort to me
I put my pain into her hands.
She gives me a purpose,
because of her I live on.
She gently erases the darkness
that has taken away any feelings of dignity.
Teresa, my search is over.
I have found, defeated my madness.
You are gone to live in my mind.
Thank you, Mother, for making me believe in,
see that dreams wash away
bring life to a broken man.
I weep no more for you, my sweet Teresa.
I rejoice in my triumphs, I belong in my home.
You are my home
that flame is eternal
as you know is my strength,
my admiration for you, Mother.

Sweet Mother

Mother, I remember you,
for all the lessons that I hold within myself.
Your gift to show me how to embrace my mistakes,
for that is when I can truly understand, find my inner beauty.
My memories are endless of you.
Bitter-sweet, somber at times that lead to tears
to reflect on the gifts that your love has given to me.
Mother, you have never left me
nor you shall ever stop embracing me.
Touching, guiding me with your driving, loving force.
Always I am your son,
forever I shall be within your heart.
You are timeless such as my love for you.
My sweet mother, this is true,
That you live such as I know
that you are one of God's most precious gifts to the world.

Until

Until the last moment I shall love you,
until truth of our love has lost its meaning.
Until all of God's promises fade and die away.
I shall hold my testament to you.
Until I cannot create and sustain my feeling for you.
Until all of heaven holds dear to God
turn away, lose its beauty.
I shall know that we are together.
Until all people lose their reason to sing and rejoice
I shall bear my sanctuary of affection to you.
Until I cannot cry in joy when you take me in your heart
Until that moment,
our moment shall never end, my sweet.

Vessel

It starts with a moment that becomes your pride,
that someone has changed your life.
When you first really respected,
cherished anything like I do you.
Look at us, God has surrendered heaven to me.
Vessel of love, you grant me a life that does not linger in
dreams.
I know your smile
how it can
touch me, to cry.
For my joy I have found.
A man is only a man with you
something more that can't be explained.
A moment that lasts forever for me
when I die to see you.
When we become one vessel.
To you, ever shall I be enraptured in your eyes.

Deeper Than

Deeper than the soul that lives inside of me.
Deeper than anything I ever felt.
Deeper than life or death,
more meaningful is the way I love you.
Deeper than any of the tears I shall ever cry.
Deeper than religion or heaven.
Deeper than my heart,
time itself
for my love is vast, boundless.
Deeper than beauty, romance,
the magic that kept us together.

Vibration

Every day I thank God for you,
the sounds of life,
the warmth of everything that I cherish.
The vibration of the earth as I lay with you
under the blanket of our loving.
Two hearts beating as one
I have found the answer to everything, you.
We are the vibration that rings out in heaven.
I look deep down into my very self,
you standing there,
greeting me to your bed of immense love.
My tears of gratitude washing away
all my doubts I have about my life.
Evermore I shall love, my dear,
gift of God, my sacred dream.

Never Say Goodbye

Never say goodbye,
I will always be inside of you
no more shall you cry
hunger for anything
for I will lay down my life for you
we shall be by no one denied happiness
or feeling not even by God.
Never say goodbye
by tears or death shall we be apart.
It is our lives where we are strong
by the bonds of love we make it through
survive so many times
I am weary in spirit
by you I always find my strength to go on
for you are always there to find.
So many words to me, but you take my hand.
I know you understand.
Never say goodbye in love
with beauty always shall we be,
never alone or apart.

For All Time

For all time beloved, my perfect song
I shall dance with you hold you tight
till we are a fond memory to the earth.
For all time we shall be called lovers,
For all times as deep as the ocean fragrant
tender is my love for you.
Words are truth
we show that each time we make love.
As heaven envies us, rest inside my dreams
hear the wind speak my voice
I am you, you are me
till the end of time, forever,
like the stars shining, flowers blooming in the spring,
we are infinite as lovers.

Across to Jordon

I looked across to Jordon.
Walked on the waves of history.
Men finally came to know Jesus.
Love conquered hatred,
and the children saved the world.
Men changed time.
I have come into the promised land
where men learned the lesson of brotherhood,
not the malice of hatred.
I have comforted the lost people,
wiped, kissed their tears away.
Fed the multitudes, who are the children of Jesus.
I looked into the eyes of men who learned to forgive.
It was silent across Jordon
no weeping in despair by women for their children.
A new day where all walks of life slept
without the hunger in their souls.
They knew a world without judgment to our people.

Human Experience

You are what I call my human experience
all that makes up our universe.
All my respect for giving me something
that only a woman as you could give.
You are a prayer said by millions
in gratitude to God for your birth.
To me, to the world, my human experience,
the gift of my peace, my hope.
My experience to a touch,
to your ever-loving homage
from me to you.
My bleak world is so much brighter, such as my heart is full.
You confide to me by comfort.
Compassion, it's why I love you my experience,
my will.

Always in My Prayers

I prayed tonight that we will never part
I prayed we never lose our love,
respect that we always find our way back to each other
I prayed that the Lord keep us whole within his eyes.
Keep us warm in the winter of our lives.
Give us spring to comfort and drive us on in hard times.
I prayed tonight for not too many tears
only in times of happiness, like new days of birth.
If we must die, we enter glory together.
I also prayed for blessed moments to remember
like our first kiss or the words of a song that moves us
to look back in our years.
I adore you
I love you
no force on earth or heaven will change that.
I tell you this in my prayers
in our lives.

Ana's Hymn

And so it was,
God thought of the most beautiful gift to give to his creation
then you came to be.
The light of all lights that shall shine in all people,
your voice strong,
moving like bells on Christmas Eve,
heard around the world.
You honor me with your smile,
gentle, fragile, like a baby's laughter.
I bow to you, symbol of love, God's living dream.
You are words that come to life,
tears shed in joy
one of love
one of everlasting life.

Dear God

Dear God,

my love,

something so beautiful,

only could have come from your mind.

Dear God,

I had drowned in my tears

until you gave me a part of you that she is.

Dear God,

I will give you back the greatest gift you have given to me,

my life.

Without her in my arms, there is no point to live.

Dear God,

all the beauty that you have created,

the wonder, the mystery of love,

she holds and she shares with me.

The countless lives that you have given birth to,

she is your favorite, that you gave to me.

It is her that I cherish forever.

Before the Last Teardrop

I have lived my life with you so many times,
I have gazed into you,
I found a new meaning to be happy.
We have danced to our songs.
Fell into despair
but have stayed strong to our dreams.
Before the last teardrop,
I shall hold you till heaven calls us home.
There is nothing my promises have not given you.
Rest with me, my dignity, my eternal choice to be a man,
that choice you shared with me.
Our memories that have given meaning to our lives.
May God breathe in our lives.
The greatest wealth within my heart is you.
Now before the last teardrop has fallen way,
We are joined in the sky forever.
Let's dance for the earth to show humanity how a man can
love you.
Now let us pass into a dream forever.
A gift from God to us.

Hobo in the Rain

I slept out in the rain,
been stained by injustice in the world.
I have lived my life in the company of the hobos
who I saw slowly die
be forgotten, ignored by the world.
I have been engulfed by self-pity, hatred,
as I watched people change to things I don't understand.
I slept outside of mansions that reached to the sky.
I found that I could only envy them, not become like them.
I have met many like me
we walk that line
the ones who are wounded
left to die, uncared for, unloved.
I am abroad
noticed only by the ghosts that only seem to recognize me.
I am many of the beggars banquet
who live the alleyways, fixtures to time.
I am the hobo who wants to just come out of the rain.

Anita

For every piece that I lacked in myself, is filled by you.
For every special moment that I have spent in your heart.
I know you are my beautiful friend.
I know you, dear love.
For every ray of sunlight that has fallen,
made my life special
you are responsible for.
I can't lock on one word to describe you,
Because you have fulfilled,
touched my life in so many ways.
In the matter of my heart, I don't speak,
because you always know how I cherish you, Anita.

You Are

You are old songs that will live on forever in time.
You are my feelings.
You are my warmth in the night that soothes my weary head.
You are my power.
You are my heart that has found its way home to you.
You are life, you are eternity.
You are my wife, you are my children.
You are a peace that I have been long searching for.
You are my youth,
my old age that will flow on evermore.

Remember the Night

Remember the night when we shared the gift.
We conceived love within our souls,
this birth of profound love,
shall show the world how beautiful love can be,
Change – purify our lives.
We opened ourselves.
We are free,
I showed you everything I feel for you.
Our moment, we showed God,
pride, joy, conception of the heart,
every emotion was vibrant, alive as we stood witness to
heaven.
we locked in an embrace, you cried.
We surrendered to each other
remember that night; I shall, my miracle.

Soul

To my friend who I give acclaim to my soul
so much I adore you
we were strangers then
you gave birth to my world
I dwelled in night, so barren, so lonely,
then time shined, brought you to my heart
two people in harmony, never parting,
a new story for the stars to show for, all overs to envy.
I shall care for you my soul mate.
How righteous it is to love someone
never know shame of being who you are
believe, my love, anything is possible under your care
take my hand,
as we are in the presence of the Lord
our names encased in eternity.

Expression

I was not sure if there was a God
then you came into my life
there was my proof, my secret of life.
I could not find love, the power to look at myself,
to love myself.
I searched for truth, warmth of another being.
It's incredible that I have found in you
laughter, expression of emotion.
My eyes have become bright with your love.
I don't have to hurt or walk alone anymore
because I love you
you mean so much
I'm not ashamed of crying or anything anymore
you took me, my life,
and forever changed it.

Lover's Hope

Let me be the first to tell you
no words spoken on the lips of God
can ever describe how much you mean to me
let me be your first wish conceived, granted by angels.
I will not live without you.
The torch of the hearts burns deep within the faith which
you are to me.
I have no course without you
I shall drift without feeling.
Let me be the first to lay down and die
Because you said it should be so
we are songs important to infinity
always the melody
my force in my times of mirth
the light in my darkest nights on going
finding rest in the arms of my lover's hope.

Marriage of the Spirit

Words in my mind baptized by music
I tremble, succumb to your lips of wine.
I am born into your graces
of a world that I can understand.
We dance in the sun
become immortal into eternity
we are younger, ageless,
in love, two people entwined, soulful, beautiful,
my best friend, my ocean that surrounds – protects me,
the fire of love, marriage of the spirit.

Witness

Witness to all of my love
I stand to the spirit,
I give everything that is holy.
Witness to the earth
to all the known beauty
we touched, shared in our lives.
Witness to the special moments we carry in us.
We are warm witness to words that you know to believe
because my voice touches your soul.
Witness to paradise as I look at you
I am in the caring love of an angel.
Love never dies
Ages – it's forever,
just as joy tears
that we are.